ESCAPING 1
THE JOURNEY OF FONG YEE

ESCAPANDO DE LA GUARDIA ROJA:
EL VIAJE DE FONG YEE

A bilingual children's book
Un libro infantil bilingüe

Victoria Chen, Author
Neil Kohney, Illustrator

1010 PUBLISHING

www.1010Publising.com

ISBN: 978-0-9993978-9-3

Printed in the United States of America.

For my grandfather, Fong Yee (Ageo) Chen.
Para mi abuelo, Fong Yee (Ageo) Chen.

Preface

This book was inspired by my grandfather and the courageous children I work with daily who immigrated to foreign countries on their own in search of a better life. My book discusses the terrifying circumstances that caused my grandfather to leave his home, family and journey to a new land, where he knew no one and had nothing but the clothes on his back. I address how my grandfather felt arriving in a new place, as a child, where he did not speak the language and knew nothing of the customs. In the current political climate, this book serves as a tool for others to better understand the challenges that unaccompanied minors face. Hopefully you find this story as fascinating as I did when my parents and aunts shared it with me.

Victoria

Acknowledgement

I have to start by thanking my wonderful parents, Rafael and Cynthia Chen, as well as my aunts Lili and Chela. Without them, I would not have known the story or the details of my grandfather's journey. I also want to thank my beautiful and talented publisher, Nury Castillo Crawford, who inspired me to not only complete a book I began 10 years ago, but actually go through with having it published. Last, but not least, I would like to thank my three fantastic children for putting up with me when I was stressed trying to meet publishing deadlines and not complaining when I was too busy working to cook them dinner.

Once upon a time, there was a young boy named Fong Yee. He loved to play baseball and was in a club called the Young Pioneers of China. He had seven brothers and five sisters who he loved to play with on the temple playground. Fong Yee's parents had a fish and rice farm in a village named Wanchao, located in Canton, China. Every night for dinner, Fong Yee, his brothers and his sisters would go to the fish tanks and pick out which fish they wanted to eat. Fong Yee was very happy.

Érase una vez, un niño llamado Fong Yee. Le encantaba jugar béisbol y estaba en un club llamado los Jóvenes pioneros de China. Tenía siete hermanos y cinco hermanas con quienes le gustaba mucho jugar en la área de juegos del templo. Los padres de Fong Yee, tenían granjas de pescado y arroz en una aldea llamada Wanchao, localizada en Canton, China. Todas las noches, para la cena, Fong Yee, sus hermanos y hermanas iban a el tanque de pescados y escogían el pescado que querían para comer. Fong Yee era muy feliz.

One day, Fong Yee overheard his parents talking about fighting in a nearby village. Many villagers had been tortured and killed by the communist soldiers known as the Red Guard. Fong Yee's parents were worried that the Red Guard would soon come to their village. That night, Fong Yee couldn't sleep. He was also worried about the Red Guard. The stories he heard about the way the Red Guard invaded villages, tortured people, and even ate them afterwards in some sort of awful ritual were terrifying.

Unfortunately, Fong Yee's parents were correct. On December 11, 1927, the Red Guard invaded the main city of Canton, China, which at that time was known as Guangzhou. Because Fong Yee's family was not a part of the communist party, they decided to try to save their children.

Un día, Fong Yee escuchó a sus padres hablar acerca de peleas en una aldea cercana. Muchos aldeanos habían sido torturados y matados por los soldados comunistas conocidos como los Guardias Rojos. Los padres de Fong Yee estaban preocupados de que los Guardias Rojos pronto vendrían a su aldea. Esa noche, Fong Yee no pudo dormir. Él también estaba preocupado por la Guardia Roja. Las historias que había escuchado acerca de cómo la Guardia Roja invadía las aldeas, torturaban a la gente, e incluso se los comían después en algún tipo de horrible ritual, fueron espantosos.

Desafortunadamente, los padres de Fong Yee estaban en lo correcto. En 11 de llamado del 1927, la Guardia Roja invadió la ciudad cabecera de Canton, China, a la cual en esos tiempos se le conocía como Guangzhou. Como la familia de Fong Yee no era parte del partido comunista, decidieron tratar de salvar a sus hijos.

"Hurry," Fong Yee's mother said, "We must go to the port now."

The port? Fong Yee wasn't aware what was going on, but had never seen his mother look so worried. Her face was pale and her hands were visibly shaking. Fong Yee and his brothers quickly went with their mother. They didn't even have time to pack their suitcases. When they arrived at the port, Fong Yee saw many huge ships. He had no idea where any of these ships were going. On other occasions, Fong Yee had come to the port with his brothers and imagined sailing off on one of the ships to an unknown land, but this was not the way he wanted to go. He had never left his village.

Fong Yee watched as his mother divided her sons into pairs for safety reasons. Fong Yee sadly watched as his brothers boarded different ships. He barely had time to say goodbye to them and wondered if he would ever see any of them again.

"Apúrense," decía la mamá de Fong Yee, "debemos irnos al puerto ahorita." ¿El puerto? Fong Yee no sabía lo que pasaba, pero nunca había visto a su madre tan preocupada. Su cara estaba pálida y sus manos le temblaban. Fong Yee y sus hermanos rápidamente se fueron con su madre, ni siquiera tuvieron tiempo de preparar sus maletas. Cuando llegaron al puerto, Fong Yee vió muchos barcos muy grandes, no tenía idea de adonde estos barcos iban. En otras ocasiones, Fong Yee había venido al puerto con sus hermanos y se había imaginado navegando en uno de estos barcos a una tierra desconocida, pero esta no era la forma como él quería irse. Nunca había dejado su aldea.

Fong Yee observó a su madre dividiendo a sus hermanos en pares, por razones de seguridad, y con tristeza miró a sus hermanos abordar diferentes barcos. El apenas tuvo tiempo de despedirse de sus hermanos y se preguntó si algún día los vería nuevamente.

Soon it was Fong Yee's turn to board a ship with his older brother. Fong Yee was afraid. He loved his mother, father, sisters, and brothers.

"Why must I go?" Fong Yee asked, crying.

Fong Yee's mother replied, "Fong Yee, you have to be a big boy now. I promise we will come find you. I love you! Now hurry before the ship workers see us! Do as your older brother says. You must hide in a barrel and not come out until the ship stops moving."

Terrified, Fong Yee hugged his mother tightly and tried to take everything in. He knew that even though she promised she would come find him, the reality was he may never see her again. His mother smelled like the Cedrela plant and ginger to him. He loved that smell. Fong Yee did not want to let her go, but for his mother he was brave. He did as she said and followed his older brother onto the ship.

Pronto fue el turno de Fong Yee para abordar uno de los barcos con su hermano mayor. Fong Yee tenía miedo. Amaba a su madre, su padre, sus hermanos y sus hermanas.

"¿Por qué me tengo que ir?" preguntó Fong Yee llorando.

Su madre respondió, "Fong Yee, ahora tienes que ser un niño grande" Te prometo que te vamos a encontrar. ¡Te amo! Ahora, ¡apúrate antes que los trabajadores del barco nos vean! Obedece a tu hermano. Te tienes que esconder en un barril y no asomarte hasta que el barco ya no se mueva."

Aterrado, Fong Yee abrazo a su madre y trató de capturar en él lo más posible de su madre. Él sabía que, aunque su madre prometió que lo encontraría, lo más seguro era que nunca la vería nuevamente. Para él, su madre olía como la planta de Cedrela y a jengibre. Él amaba ese olor. Fong Yee no quería dejarla ir, pero por su madre, fue valiente. Hizo como ella le dijo y siguió a su hermano mayor al barco.

Fong Yee boarded the ship with his brother. They found barrels to hide in. It was dark and smelled of tea inside. Fong Yee felt cramped. His mother had given him some wantons, shrimp dumplings, and water, but Fong Yee had no idea how long he would be in this barrel. Where was this boat even going? Fong Yee sobbed softly as the ship started moving. The strong odor of tea inside the barrel made him feel sick to his stomach. He tried to distract his mind by thinking of one day reuniting with his family and playing on the playground with his brothers and sisters. Fong Yee did not want to throw up inside the barrel because he did not know when he would get out of it and had no change of clothes. He felt like he had spent weeks cramped inside that barrel, when in reality it had been a little under a day.

Fong Yee abordó el barco con su hermano, y encontraron barriles para esconderse. Estaba oscuro y por dentro los barriles olían a té. Fong Yee se sentía apretado. Su madre le había dado algunos wantons, dumplings de camarón, y agua, pero Fong Yee no tenía idea de cuánto tiempo estaría metido en este barril. ¿A dónde iba este barco? Cuando el barco comenzó a moverse Fong Yee empezó a sollozar. El fuerte olor a té adentro del barril hizo que el estómago se le revolviera. Trató de distraer su mente imaginándose que un día se reuniría nuevamente con su familia y jugaría en el área de juegos con sus hermanos y hermanas. Fong Yee no quería vomitar adentro del barril porque no sabía cuándo podría salir de él y no tenía ropa para cambiarse. Sentía que tenía semanas confinado en este barril, cuando apenas había pasado menos de un día.

After what seemed like an eternity to Fong Yee, the ship stopped and he got out of his barrel. He felt very weak and his legs were wobbly. He had to brace himself to keep from falling as he made his way off the ship. It was very loud outside. There were many people and many rice boats. Fong Yee looked off into the distance and saw beautiful green mountains. He wished he could go home. Fong Yee's thoughts of home were interrupted by his brother.

"Hurry," his older brother exclaimed. "We have to board this ship that is going to Panama."

Once again, Fong Yee felt his stomach drop. Another ship? He barely had any food left. Would he have to hide in a barrel again? Where was Panama? How did his brother even know which boat was going there? Reluctantly, Fong Yee followed his brother and boarded the ship headed to Panama. The ship was very crowded, but Fong Yee was relieved he did not have to hide in another barrel.

Luego de lo que a Fong Yee pareció una eternidad, el barco se detuvo y pudo salir del barril. Se sentía débil y sus piernas temblorosas. Tuvo que hacer uso de todas sus fuerzas para no caer mientras caminaba alejándose del barco. Afuera había mucho ruido, había mucha gente y muchos barcos arroceros. Fong Yee miró a la distancia y vio unas hermosas montañas verdes, deseo poder regresar a casa, pero sus pensamientos fueron interrumpidos por su hermano

"Apúrate," le decía. "Tenemos que abordar este barco que va a Panamá." Una vez más Fong Yee sintió que su estómago se le revolvía. ¿otro barco? Ya casi no le quedaba comida. ¿tendría que esconderse nuevamente en un barril? ¿dónde quedaba Panamá? Incluso, ¿cómo su hermano sabía cuál barco se dirigía a Panamá? De mala gana, Fong Yee siguió a su hermano y abordo el barco que se dirigía a Panamá. El barco estaba lleno de gente, pero Fong Yee se sintió aliviado de que no tenía que esconderse en otro barril.

During the first few days on the ship, Fong Yee was seasick. Around the third day he began to feel better. Several families were on the ship and they all shared their food, which was mostly seaweed, sardines, and rice. Fong Yee began to lose track of the days that passed. Finally, Fong Yee saw land! He hoped this was his final stop and that he never had to get on a ship again!

Durante los primeros días en el barco, Fong Yee estuvo mareado. Pero, alrededor del tercer día comenzó a sentirse mejor. Había varias familias en el barco y ellas compartían sus alimentos, lo cual consistía mayormente de algas marinas, sardinas, y arroz. Fong Yee comenzó a perder el sentido de los días que habían trascurrido. Finalmente, Fong Yee vio tierra y deseó que éste sea el destino final y que ¡nunca tenga que subirse a otro barco.

A few hours later, the ship docked. Fong Yee and his brother got off the boat. Once again, Fong Yee's legs felt wobbly, and he was a bit unsteady as he began walking on solid ground. The air was hot and muggy. It felt like summertime in his village. Suddenly, Fong Yee and his brother were surrounded by people. He had no idea what they were saying. They were all speaking in a language that he had never heard before. They looked different, too. Fong Yee felt scared and lost. He followed his brother and the other families from the boat. They had to sign some papers.

Fong Yee's brother told him, "In this new country, we must use a new name. Your new name is Ageo." Fong Yee did not want to change his name. His parents had given him his name and he liked his name. Fong Yee began to protest. "Fong Yee", his brother said, "we do not have time for this foolishness. Your new name is Ageo and that is the end of it." Fong Yee remembered the promise he had made to his mother to listen to his brother. "Okay," he replied reluctantly.

Unas horas más tarde, el barco atracó. Fong Yee y su hermano bajaron del barco. Una vez más, las piernas de Fong Yee estaban temblorosas y un poco inestables cuando comenzó a caminar en tierra firme. El aire estaba caliente y húmedo, parecido al verano en su aldea. De pronto, Fong Yee y su hermano estaban rodeados de gente. No tenía idea de lo que decían, todos estaban hablando en un idioma que nunca había escuchado, y se miraban diferente también. Fong Yee se sintió temeroso y perdido. Siguió a su hermano y a las otras familias del barco. Tenían que firmar unos papeles.

Su hermano le dijo, "En este nuevo país, necesitaremos usar un nuevo nombre. Tu nuevo nombre es Ageo." Fong Yee no quería cambiarse el nombre, sus padres le habían escogido su nombre y a el le gustaba su nombre. Fong Yee comenzó a protestar, pero su hermano le dijo, "Fong Yee", "no tenemos tiempo para estas tonterías. Tu nuevo nombre es Ageo y eso es todo. "Fong Yee recordó la promesa que le había hecho a su madre de obedecer a su hermano. "Ok," respondió de mala gana.

Fong Yee and his older brother got into a truck with their newfound friends. Fong Yee was exhausted and soon fell asleep. When he woke up, his brother told him they would soon arrive at a village. His brother called the village Sona. All Fong Yee knew was that he was starving. He hoped there was food in Sona.

Fong Yee y su hermano se subieron a la camioneta junto con sus nuevos amigos. Fong Yee estaba exhausto y se durmió. Cuando despertó, su hermano le dijo que pronto llegarían a la aldea, a la cual su hermano llamó Sona. Todo lo que Fong Yee sabia era que se moría de hambre y deseo que en Sona hubiera comida.

Fong Yee and the others arrived at a house in Sona. The house was owned by an older woman from Fong Yee's home village. He thought she looked a little bit like his grandmother and he instantly liked her. Her name was Seng Lee and she smiled as she greeted Fong Yee and his brother. Fong Yee noticed that she was missing her bottom teeth. "Welcome to Panama," she said. "Please come in and have something to eat. You boys must be starving." Fong Yee was famished, and Seng Lee's cooking was similar to his mothers. For a brief moment, he forgot all about his fear of life in this unknown country.

Fong Yee y los otros llegaron a una casa en Sona. La dueña de la casa era una mujer mayor de la aldea de Fong Yee. Pensó que se parecía un poco a su abuelita e inmediatamente le calló bien. La mujer se llamaba Seng Lee, y sonreía mientras los recibía a su hermano y a él. Fong Yee notó que le faltaban los dientes de abajo. Ella dijo "Bienvenidos a Panamá. Por favor pasen a comer algo, se deben estar muriendo de hambre." Fong Yee estaba hambriento, y la comida de Seng Lee se parecía a la de su mamá. Por un pequeño instante, se olvidó de su miedo a la vida en este nuevo país.

After dinner, Fong Yee, his brother, and the others sat down to discuss their next steps. Fong Yee and his brother would get pots and pans made in Sona and take them to the capital city to sell. Fong Yee missed home. He did not want to sell pots and pans. He wanted to go back home and play baseball with his friends in his village. Later, when it was time to go to sleep, Fong Yee told his brother how he felt.

"I know you miss home, Fong Yee," his brother said, "but we do not even know if our village is still there. The soldiers may have destroyed it. This is our life now. We must do as we are told and sell these pots to earn money. One day, we will return home to our village." Fong Yee was sad, but listened to his brother.

Después de la cena, Fong Yee, su hermano y otros se sentaron a hablar de sus siguientes pasos. Fong Yee y su hermano tomarían ollas y sartenes hechos en Sona y los llevarían a vender a la capital. Fong Yee extrañaba su casa, no quería vender ollas y sartenes. El quería volver a casa y jugar béisbol con sus amigos de la aldea.

Más tarde, a la hora de dormir, Fong Yee le dijo a su hermano como se sentía, "ya sé que extrañas nuestra casa Fong Yee," le contestó su hermano, "pero ni siquiera sabemos si nuestra aldea exista" quizás los soldados la destruyeron. Esta es nuestra vida. Debemos hacer lo que nos dicen y vender estas ollas para ganar dinero. Un día, regresaremos a nuestra aldea. Fong Yee estaba triste, pero escuchó a su hermano.

Fong Yee started off selling pots and pans, and later cows and pigs. Years later, he earned enough money to buy himself a rice farm like the one his parents had back in Wanchao. He married a woman he met in Sona named Rubi, and together they raised five children. Later, Fong Yee started his own rice brand and named the rice he manufactured, Rubi S.A., after his wife. He was considered successful, and sent his four daughters and son to the university. Fong Yee felt it was very important for his daughters to have a college education. His views were uncommon for a man of his time. He sometimes dreamt of his home in China. He knew his father had been tortured and killed by the Red Guard shortly after he escaped his village. His mother passed away a few years later. Although Fong Yee was sad that he would never see his parents again, he tried to make the best of his new life with his own family.

Fong Yee comenzó a vender ollas y sartenes, despues vacas y cerdos. Años después, gano suficiente dinero para comprarse una granja de arroz como la que tenían sus padres antes en Wanchao. Se casó con una mujer que conoció en Sona de nombre Rubí y juntos tuvieron cinco hijos. Más tarde, Fong Yee comenzó su propia marca de arroz y a la manufacturera le puso el nombre de Rubí, S. A., por su esposa. Él era considerado una persona de éxito y mandó a sus cuatro hijas y su hijo a la universidad. Fong Yee sentía que era muy importante que sus hijas tuvieran una educación universitaria. Sus puntos de vista no eran comunes de un hombre en esos tiempos. A veces, soñaba en su hogar. Supo que su padre fue torturado y asesinado por los Guardias Rojos poco después de que él escapara de la aldea. Su madre murió unos años después. Aunque Fong Yee se sentía triste de que nunca mas volvería a ver a sus padres, el trató de hacer lo mejor de su nueva vida con su propia familia.

About sixty years after the day Fong Yee boarded that ship in the port of his village, he was finally able to return to Wanchao. He was in his seventies and now an old man. Fong Yee expected that his village and his home would no longer be standing, and had mentally prepared himself to face the fact that nothing would look the same. Fong Yee assumed everything had been destroyed by the communist soldiers. He also did not expect to find any of his family members still alive.

When Fong Yee arrived at his old village of Wanchao, he could not believe it! The temple he used to go to with his family was still standing! So was the park behind the temple where he played baseball with his brothers and sisters. Fong Yee turned the corner. There was his old house still intact and the fish tanks where he used to pick out the fish he wanted for dinner were still there with fish inside them! Fong Yee was very emotional.

Cerca de sesenta años después de que Fong Yee abordara el barco en el puerto de su aldea, finalmente él pudo regresar a Wanchao. Estaba en los setenta años de edad y esperaba que su aldea y su casa no existirían más, así que se preparó mentalmente para enfrentar el hecho de que nada se miraría igual. Fong Yee asumió que todo había sido destruido por los soldados comunistas y no esperaba encontrar a nadie de su familia con vida.

Cuando Fong Yee llegó a su vieja aldea Wanchao, ¡no lo podía creer! El templo al que solía asistir con su familia. ¡Todavía estaba en pie! al igual que el parque en la parte trasera en donde jugaba béisbol con sus hermanos y hermanas. Fong Yee dio vuelta a la esquina, y ahí estaba su casa, todavía intacta, y también el estanque de los peces en donde el eligió su pescado para la cena y ¡Aún había pescados ahí! Fong Yee se puso muy emocional.

Fong Yee was shaking as he knocked on the door of his old home. Fong Yee's sister answered. It had been over sixty years since Fong Yee last saw her. Memories came flooding back and he could no longer contain his emotions. He sobbed as he hugged his only living sister. She invited him inside. He stood in the doorway of his old home in amazement. All of the furniture Fong Yee remembered as a child was still there! For a minute, it seemed as if he had never left. Fong Yee sat down on the sofa he sat on sixty years ago. He was so happy to be home!

After visiting with his sister for three months, Fong Yee returned to Panama where he lived with his wife, Rubi, and his daughters until he passed away at the age of ninety-nine.

Fong Yee estaba temblando cuando tocó a la puerta de su vieja casa. La hermana de Fong Yee abrió la puerta. Habían pasado más de sesenta años desde que Fong Yee la vio. Los recuerdos vinieron a su memoria y no pudo contener más la emoción. Lloro mientras abrazaba a su única hermana con vida. Ella lo invitó a pasar. El se quedó parado en la puerta de la casa maravillado. Todos los muebles que Fong Yee recordaba de niño ¡Ahí estaban! parecía que nunca se hubiera ido. Fong Yee se sentó en el sofá en donde se sentó hace sesenta años. ¡Se sentía tan feliz de estar en casa!

Después de quedarse visitando a su hermana por tres meses, Fong Yee regresó a Panamá donde vivío con su esposa Rubí y sus hijas hasta que falleció a la edad de noventa y nueve.

Epilogue

Just like Fong Yee, many children come to the United States every day seeking an education, wanting a better life, or fleeing violence. These children come with no parents. Many of them are orphans. They are called "unaccompanied minors". They are taken in by immigration when they cross the border and are placed in shelters until a sponsor can be located for them.

Así como Fong Yee, muchos niños vienen a los Estados Unidos cada día buscando educación, deseando una mejor vida o huyendo de la violencia. Estos niños llegan sin padres, muchos de ellos son huerfanos. Se les llama "menores sin compania". Ellos son recogidos por imigración cuando pasan la frontera y se les lleva a refugios hasta que se encuentre a un patrocinador para ellos.

About the Author

Victoria Chen was born in Cuyahoga Falls, Ohio, but grew up in the Republic of Panama. At the age of 21, she moved back to the United States where she graduated from the State University of New York with a B.A. in Psychology. She later relocated to Atlanta where she worked in a small private school. This sparked her interest to return to school for teaching. She received her M. Ed in Administration and Supervision and taught early childhood education (Pre-K – grade 5) for about 10 years. She then decided she wanted to work with children in a different capacity and decided to return to school for her MSW. She graduated and obtained her LMSW four months later

Victoria has worked as a teacher, a benefits caseworker, a domestic violence legal advocate, and an unaccompanied minor's caseworker. Her passion lies in assisting immigrants, refugees, and children.

Victoria is the mother of three children; a girl and two boys. She enjoys spending time outdoors; either at the beach, hiking, or running.

Made in the USA
Columbia, SC
26 January 2022

54848412R00022